THE PRISONER AND DANGER MAN COLLECTIBLES

John Buss

AMBERLEY

Acknowledgements

I would like to thank the following for their assistance in the preparation of this book. Louise Harker at Vectis Toy Auctions. Remco Admiraal for assistance in tracking down many of the European items that otherwise would have escaped me. Jaz Wiseman, Rick Davy of the www.theunmutual.co.uk website, Matt Courtman of www.danger-man.co.uk website, and Martin Gainsford for allowing me to use the story from his previously published interview. Thanks to Bernard Dunne, Phil Caunt and Brian Nightingale. Also thanks to the Little Storping Museum website, www.murdersville.co.uk/museum. Finally, thanks to William Woodward for his help and proofreading skills.

First published 2021

Amberley Publishing
The Hill, Stroud
Gloucestershire, GL5 4EP

www.amberley-books.com

Copyright © John Buss, 2021

The right of John Buss to be identified as the Author of this work has been asserted in accordance with the Copyrights, Designs and Patents Act 1988.

ISBN 978 1 3981 0131 9 (print)
ISBN 978 1 3981 0132 6 (ebook)

British Library Cataloguing in Publication Data.
A catalogue record for this book is available from the British Library.

Typeset in 10pt on 13pt Celeste.
Typesetting by SJmagic DESIGN SERVICES, India.
Printed in the UK.

Contents

Introduction

Danger Man and *The Prisoner* are two shows forever linked by their enigmatic star Patrick McGoohan. Are the shows linked? Well, both were made by Sir Lew Grades ITC TV Company, and McGoohan played a man with a top-secret job in both shows. Would *The Prisoner* have been created and made had *Danger Man* not existed first? Who can tell? Undoubtedly, *The Prisoner's* village location was inspired by McGoohan's visit to Portmeirion in 1959 while filming an early episode of *Danger Man*. Some would also argue that since it is McGoohan's publicity photograph for *Danger Man* that is struck through in the opening credits of *The Prisoner*, that both characters are one and the same (though the photograph was not taken specifically for the series, it was, however, the one sent out by the studio for that series). *The Prisoner* throws up many questions, but it is in the minds of many inextricably linked to *Danger Man*. It is not the intention of this book to explore these questions, but it is an exploration of collectibles from both series.

Danger Man AKA *Secret Agent*

Danger Man first aired in September 1960 and arguably kicked off the spy craze on television of that decade. The series followed the exploits of John Drake, an agent working for the secret service branch of NATO. Early on this was a fairly routine spy adventure series, with Drake facing different assignments each week in any part of the world (or part of the studio backlot). The series was originally a half-hour black and white show, thirty-nine episodes being made in this format. While the show was relatively popular that might have remained it had the James Bond movies not become a cinematic hit.

After a gap of several years the show was revived in 1964, now in an hour-long format. With the advent of this also came the secret gadgets and spy equipment (must keep up with Mr Bond). There was also a change in Drake's boss, for he no longer worked for NATO, but instead MI9. Drake was very much a loner in complete charge of any assignment he tackled. In total a further forty-seven episodes were produced in this hour-long format, with the final two being made in colour in 1966.

The show's star, Patrick McGoohan, became an international star as a result of this series and subsequently went on to create and star in *The Prisoner*.

The half-hour episodes appear to have been shown in the USA sometime during 1961 under their original UK title of *Danger Man*. The second batch of hour-long episodes, however, underwent a name change and the series was known as *Secret Agent* when they were broadcast in North America, complete with a new theme song sung by Johnny Rivers. This name change only ever effected the hour-long episodes of the show.

A note on this series for American readers: this series was only ever known as *Danger Man* in the UK, henceforth any items that were issued in the UK under the name Secret Agent do not relate to this series, but were the manufacturer's attempt to cash in on the spy craze during this period, without having to pay one of the TV companies to use their character.

Books

Paperbacks

Consul Books, a division of World Distributors Ltd, published five novels based upon the series in the UK. The first three published in 1965 at a price of *3s 6d* were *Departure Deferred*, *Storm over Rockall* and *Hell for Tomorrow*. The first two were written by W. Howard Baker, with the third being written by Peter Leslie, a prolific writer of TV tie-ins, penning two *Avengers* novels with Patrick Macnee, as well as *Man from U.N.C.L.E.*, *The Invaders* and *Daktari* novels to name but a few. The next two novels were *No Way Out* and *The Exterminator*, published in 1966, written by Wilfred McNeilly and W.A. Ballinger respectively. There was a later edition of *The Exterminator*, which had all references to the TV series removed from the cover.

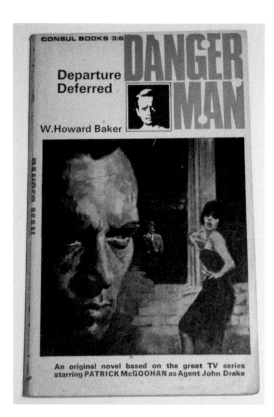

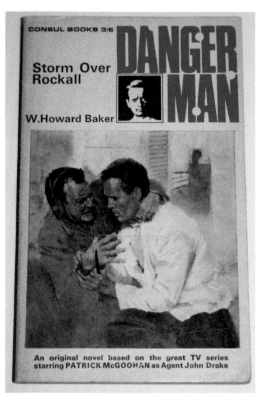

Above left: UK paperback *Departure Deferred*.

Above right: UK paperback *Storm over Rockall*.

Left: UK paperback *Hell for Tomorrow*.

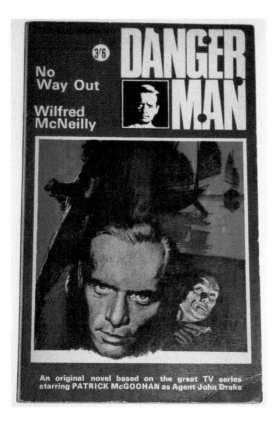

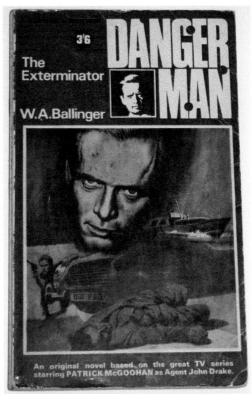

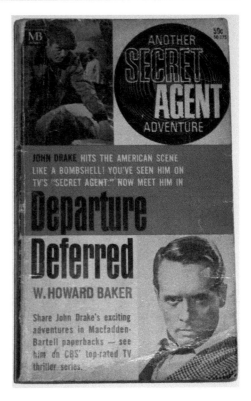

Above left: UK paperback *No Way Out*.

Above right: UK paperback *The Exterminator*.

Right: USA paperback *Departure Deferred*.

Above left: USA paperback *Storm over Rockall.*

Above right: USA paperback *Hell for Tomorrow.*

Left: USA paperback *No Way Out.*

Above left: USA paperback *The Exterminator*.

Above right: USA paperback *Target for Tonight*.

All five of these novels also saw publication in the USA under the American title for the series *Secret Agent*, being published by the firm Macfadden Bartell and priced at 50 cents each. The first four titles saw release in 1966, while the final one, *The Exterminator*, was published in 1967. Interestingly a sixth novel also appeared in the USA four years earlier, during the run of half-hour-long episodes in February 1962. This was not a *Secret Agent* product as with almost all American merchandise for the show, but a *Danger Man* novel titled *Target for Tonight*. This was published by Dell Publishing Co. and was written by Richard Telfair. It is quite possibly the only novel to be based upon the earlier half-hour incarnation of the series.

Danger Man was immensely popular around the world. In France the series was known as *Destination Danger,* and all five of the UK paperbacks saw publication, though in a completely different order. The first four to be published were produced by Solar Books in their *Tele Roman* range. *The Exterminator* by W.A. Ballinger was the first of the series being published in 1967 and translated into French by Constance Gallet. The following three titles were all published in 1968, having been translated by Marie Watkins. These were *Storm over Rockall* by W. Howard Baker, translated as *Sabotage et Cafouillage. No Way Out* by Wilfred McNeilly became *Manigances a Macao*, while Peter Leslie's novel *Hell for Tomorrow* was published as *L'enfer est pour demain.*

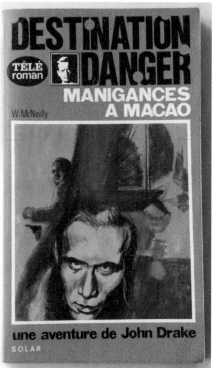

Above left: French paperback.

Above right: French paperback.

Left: French paperback.

Above left: French paperback.

Above right: French paperback.

The fifth and final of these French editions causes some confusion. *Chinoiseries en Albaine*, published in 1969 by *Presses De La Cite*, according to the details inside the cover, appears to be a translation of *Departure Deferred* by W. Howard Baker, which was the first of the UK books, being translated into French by Othenin Girard. The cover, though, confusingly gives the name of John Long. The relevance of this name is a mystery, as the character is still known as John Drake in the French version of the series and it seems to bear no relationship to either the original author or the translator.

In Spain three *Agente Secreto* paperbacks appear to have been published, which were all issued by Editorial Fher at a price of 20 pesetas each in 1966. The first of these was *The Exterminator,* or *El Exterminador,* to give it its Spanish title, by W.A. Ballinger, which was followed by *No Way Out,* which became *Sin Salida* by Wilfred McNeilly. Then thirdly *Storm over Rockall* by W. Howard Baker became *Tormenta Sobre Rockall.*

Three books were also published in Portugal by publishers Deaga. W. H. Baker's *Departure Deferred* became *Partida adiada,* while *No Way Out* by Wilfred McNeilly translated as *Sem nenhuma saida* and the Peter Leslie penned *Hell for Tomorrow* saw release as *Inferno Para Amanha.*

In Germany where the series appears to have been called *Geheimauftrag fur John Drake* there appear to be two paperbacks published by Signum Taschenbucher. The first title released by the firm appears to be *Geheimauftrag fur John Drake Mord Auf Bestellung,*

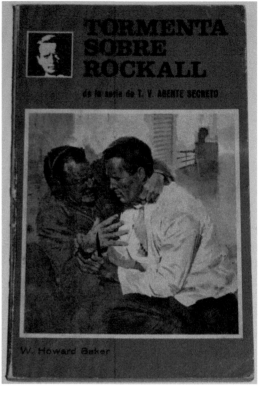

Above left: Spanish paperback.
(Bernard Dunne)

Above right: Spanish paperback.

Left: Spanish paperback. (Bernard Dunne)

Above left: Portuguese paperback.
(Jaz Wiseman)

Above right: Portuguese paperback.
(Jaz Wiseman)

Right: Portuguese paperback.
(Jaz Wiseman)

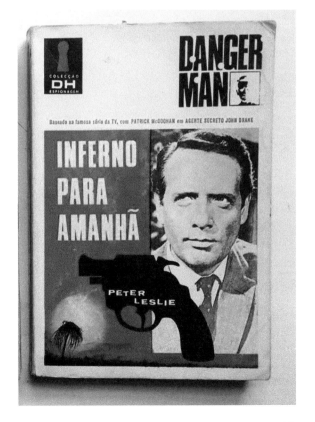

which translates as *Secret Task for John Drake Murder on Order*. This is by Ralph Smart and appears to be the only publication of this story. There is no publication date given within the book, though translation details are given as being translated from English by Wolfgang Lohmann. From studying the back cover it looks like there may have been a second title in this series: *Gasthof zum Galgen*. Strangely this second title doesn't appear to translate into English.

German
paperback.

W.A. BALLINGER

DE KLINISCHE UITROEIER

'Danger Man' John Drake contra een beroepsmoordenaar die zich verscholen kan hebben onder de voor niets

DANGER MAN

①

terugdeinzende bemanning van een miljonairsjacht of achter de rotsblokken op de gloeiende hellingen van de Etna-vulkaan . . .

BORN POCKETS

MYSTERIES

Dutch paperback. (Remco Admiraal)

WILFRED McNEILLY

OPDRACHT ZONDER UITWEG

'Danger Man' John Drake aan de grens van Rood-China, speurend naar zijn roekeloze, spoorloos verdwenen collega Tony Harris, met de bittere opdracht hem te ontvoeren of . . . te doden! En Tony Harris is zijn vriend . . .

DANGER MAN 2

MYSTERIES

Dutch paperback. (Remco Admiraal)

16

Paperbacks also appeared in the Netherlands where Born NV Uitgeversmaatschappij were the publishers of two titles. The first was *Danger Man De Klinische uitroeier*, which was a translation of *The Exterminator* by W. A. Ballinger, having been translated by T. de Hau. The second *Danger Man 2 Opdracht zonder uitweg* (*No Way Out*) by Wilfred McNeilly was translated by G.W. de Roos. Both titles were published in 1968 and featured covers designed by Alex Jagtenberg.

Two paperbacks were also published in Danish in 1971. These were published by Winthers Forlag. The first was *John Drake: hemmelig agent Danger Man 1*

Above left: Israeli paperback. (Jaz Wiseman)

Above right: Israeli paperback. (Jaz Wiseman)

Right: Israeli paperback. (Jaz Wiseman)

Above left: Israeli paperback.
(Jaz Wiseman)

Above right: Japanese paperback.
(Bernard Dunne)

Left: Japanese paperback reverse.
(Bernard Dunne)

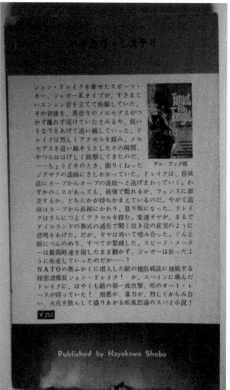

Likvideringseksperten, E. Eskestad translating *The Exterminator* by W. A. Ballinger. P. Borch translated *John Drake: Hemnelig agent Danger Man 2 Døde agenter taler ikke*, which had started life as *Departure Deferred* by W. H. Baker.

All five *Danger Man* paperbacks appear to have been released in Israel, while Japan also saw the issue of at least one paperback for the series. This was the 1962 novel *Target for Tonight* by Richard Telfair, which, while it was a paperback edition, did have a photographic dust jacket. This having been published by Hayakawa Shobo.

Annual and Hardbacks

Four of the *Danger Man* stories published in the UK were released in hardback omnibus editions by Howard Baker Publishing Ltd in 1968. *The First Dangerman Omnibus* contained *The Exterminator* by W. A. Ballinger and *Departure Deferred* by W. H. Baker, while *The Second Dangerman Omnibus* contained Wilfred McNeilly's *No Way Out* and W. H. Baker's *Storm over Rockall*.

Young World Productions Ltd produced two hardbacks based on *Danger Man* in 1965. Issued as *Top TV Series Starring Dangerman*. Both of the two books produced in the series were forty-eight paged annual sized hardbacks containing two black and white strip stories. The first of them was called *War against the Mafia*. The cover of this book is red with a small photograph of John Drake and a colour illustration from the story. Interestingly, at least the title story appears to have been licenced from a French publisher, as this story does appear in a French *Thierry La Fronde* comic from a year earlier, so it is quite probable

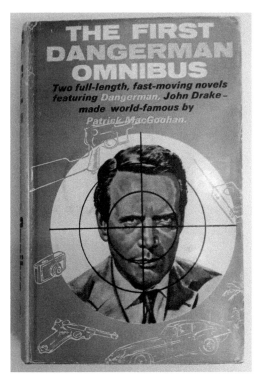

Above left: UK first omnibus. (Matt Courtman, www.danger-man.co.uk)

Above right: UK second omnibus. (Matt Courtman, www.danger-man.co.uk)

Top TV Series War Against the Mafia.

War Against the Mafia title page.

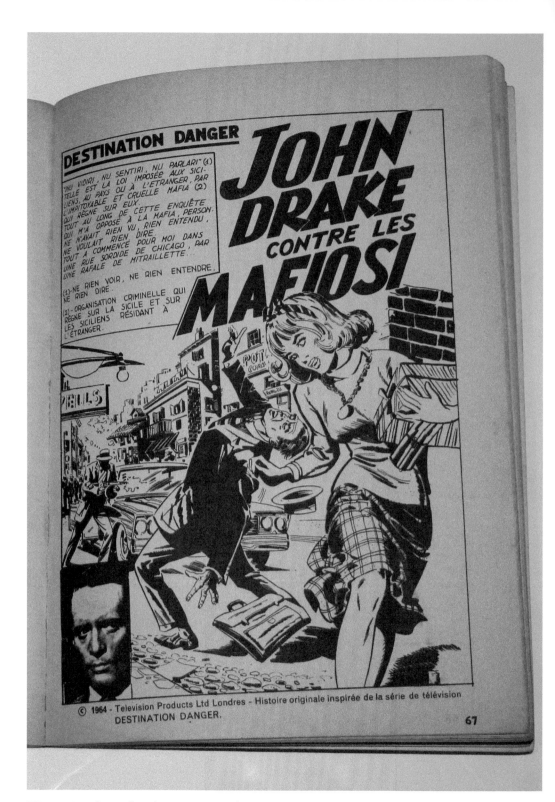

War against the Mafia title page in French.

Top TV Series
Kingdom of Fear.

that the other *Danger Man* stories used in these two books came from the same source, though this has not yet been confirmed.

The second *Top TV Series starring Dangerman* book was titled *Kingdom of Fear* and featured a cover very similar in appearance to the other book in this series.

Danger Man Annual (© 1965. Year not on cover)

World Distributors Ltd published two annuals based on the series. The first appeared in 1965 and this features a dark blue cover, with a black spine. The front cover shows a drawing of John Drake in the bottom left corner, and in the background is an aircraft, with a man running from this, holding a briefcase. The pilot is chasing him while a helicopter hovers overhead. The back cover is also dark blue with a head and shoulders drawing of Drake in the middle. This artwork is believed to be by Walt Howarth, a prolific artist whose work graced many classic World Distributors annuals throughout the 1960s and 1970s. This annual, published at an original price of 9s 6d, contained a selection of text stories and features based upon the series. Some of the stories included *The Big Catch, Traitor's*

23

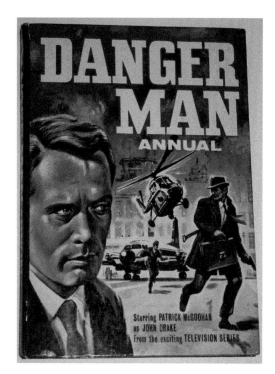

Above left: *Danger Man Annual* 1965.

Above right: *Danger Man Annual* 1966.

Gate, The House on 22nd Street, and *Night Train To Rome,* while features included *The Code Crackers, Half a Million in a World Spy Ring* and *Beat This Dangerman Code.*

Danger Man Annual (© 1966. Year not on cover)

The second World Distributors Ltd annual appeared the following year. The cover of this annual is black with a yellow spine. The centre of the cover is like a target, with a head

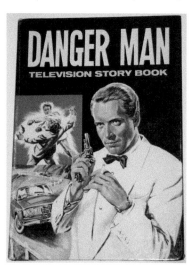

Danger Man Television Story Book.

and shoulders drawing of Drake in the centre. Surrounding this are white line drawings, starting at the top in a clockwise direction. They are a sniper's rifle, a radio, a palm tree and man, a Jaguar car, a gun and a camera. The back cover shows a white line drawing of a man being chased by a helicopter. Once again it is believed that the artwork may be by Walt Howarth. This annual contains text stories, some of which are *The Big Splash*, *No Medals for the General*, *The Silver Ring*, and *Smoke Out!* The original price for this annual was 10*s* 6*d*.

Danger Man Television Story Book
A further annual-sized book, published by PBS Ltd in 1965, was issued for the series. The *Danger Man Television Story Book* was predominantly text stories, the cover once again featuring Walt Howarth art, this time an image of John Drake dressed in a white jacket with black bow tie. To the left of this are two smaller drawings. The top drawing shows Drake hitting an opponent, while the bottom one shows a car chase. The background is black and the book has a red spine. Both the back and front covers show the same images. Some of the stories contained included *Trouble in Paradise, Gold Hat, Drake Takes A Bow* and *The Girl on the M6*. The single feature within this book is *How Observant Are You?*

Two annuals appear to have also been translated and published in Portugal by Livraria Civilização. The first of these two Portuguese editions features the same grey cover artwork as the first UK omnibus. It contains short stories that appear to be translations of the

Above left: Portuguese annual. (Bernard Dunne)

Above right: Portuguese annual. (© Rick Davy, www.theunmutual.co.uk)

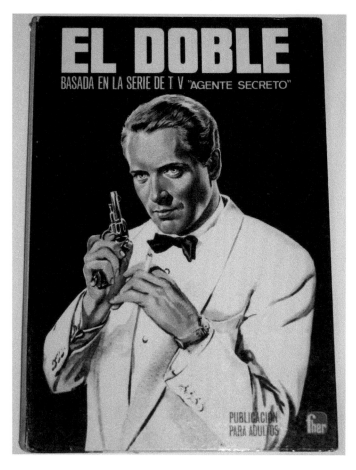

Spanish annual.

text stories featured in the British annuals minus the illustrations. The second Portuguese annual also appears to contain further text stories from the British annuals but once again minus the illustrations used in those annuals. This annual has the same cover artwork, but on the black background as with the UK annual.

In Spain the book *El Doble Basada en la serie de TV 'Agente Secreto'* appeared published by Fher. This book is mostly a translation of the PBS Ltd *Danger Man Television Picture Story book* featuring much of the same Howarth artwork and stories as the original, though the stories contained have been reordered from the UK publication. It is also interesting to note the small print on the books front cover 'Publicacion para Adultos' ('Publication for adults'). The UK equivalent book was most definitely aimed at a teenage market, but in Spain it seems this was deemed adult material.

Asides from these publications, which were produced to directly connect to the TV series, several other publications also featured the series within their pages.

Possibly the first publication to feature anything on the series was the *ATV Television Star Book* (© 1961), published by Purnell, which contained a five-page feature on *Danger Man* and its star Patrick McGoohan.

More notable, however, was the *TV Crimebusters* book, which was published by TV Publications Ltd in 1962. This annual sized book contained a *Danger Man* strip, which

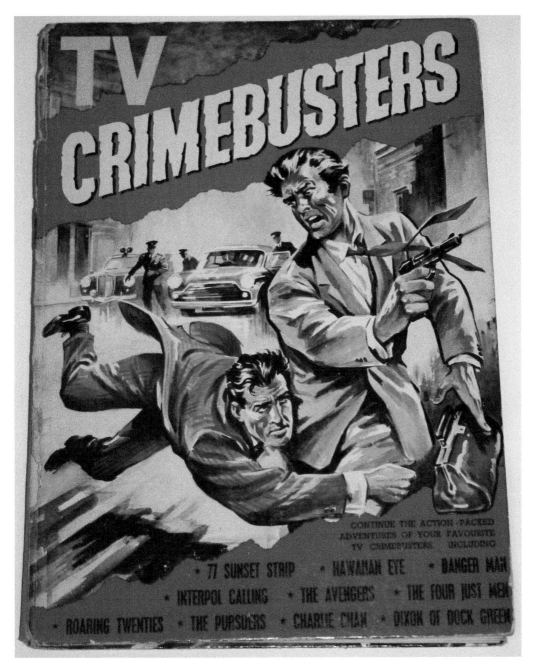

TV Crimebusters Annual.

is probably the first strip story to have been based on the series, the stories in *TV Express* comic all being text-based stories. It is also interesting for the combined use of photographs and illustrations in the production of this strip story. This annual sized book priced at 8*s* 6*d* also used the same technique for similar strip stories of other shows such as *The Avengers*.

Danger Man strip from *TV Crimebusters Annual.*

The Publishers Purnell featured Patrick McGoohan in the *ATV Television Star Book* (© 1963). This annual sized book contained references to *Danger Man* in an article with photographs of McGoohan in *Danger Man*.

In the following years *Television Star Book* (© 1964), again published by Purnell, Patrick McGoohan would again feature in the contents, alongside other stars and TV shows of the

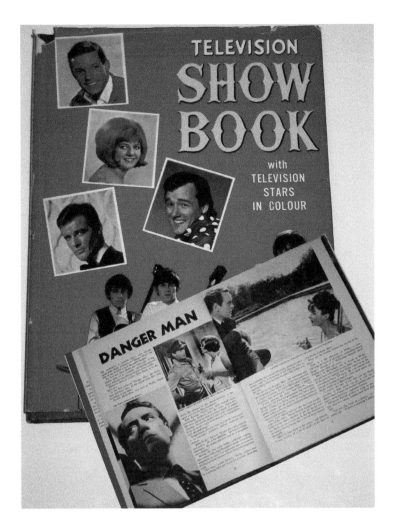

Television Show Book.

period such as Patrick Macnee (*The Avengers*) and Roger Moore (*The Saint*). The original price for this annual in 1964 was 5s. All three of these series would also feature in Purnell's more expensive (a whole 10s 6d, over double the cost) *Television Show Book* (© 1964) in the same year.

The next year Purnell's *Television Show Book* (© 1965) once again featured *Danger Man* with a four-page article on the series. While *Girl Film & Television Annual 1965* from Odhams Books would include McGoohan and *Danger Man* in a feature on television heroes.

Danger Man would feature on the cover of Purnell's *Television Stars* (© 1966), the colour dust jacket having photographs not only of *Danger Man*, but also *The Man from U.N.C.L.E.* and others. This particular Purnell book is a treasure trove of classic 1960s television, containing photographs and features on not only *Danger Man*, but also *The Man from U.N.C.L.E.*, *The Avengers*, *The Baron*, *The Saint*, *Lost in Space* (photo only), *The Fugitive*, *Thunderbirds*, Daleks (*Doctor Who*), plus many other TV shows of the time. The *Boyfriend Book 1966* saw fit to print photographs of both Patrick McGoohan and Roger Moore, *Danger Man* and *The Saint* respectively, but strangely did not include any other material on either series.

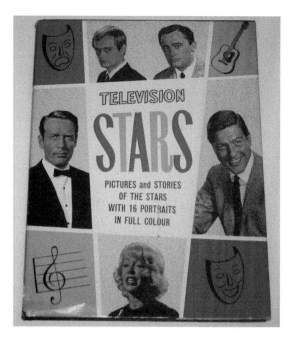 

Above left: Television Stars Book.

Above right: Ranger Book 1967.

An untitled eight-page-long *Danger Man* strip story, illustrated by Ernest Ratcliff, featured in the *Ranger Book 1967,* from Fleetway publications, published at an original price of 12*s* 6*d*. The same year Patrick McGoohan and *Danger Man* featured as part of an article in *Star TV & Film Annual 1967*, from Odhams Books.

The girls' comic *Diana* included small references to *Danger Man*, as well as other spy shows such as *The Avengers* and *The Man from U.N.C.L.E* in its 1968 annual.

Games and Puzzles

Unlike many of its contemporaries very little in the way of toys and games were issued for *Danger Man* in the 1960s. While several secret agent type toy guns or gun sets, along with other generic secret agent type products, were produced by various manufactures during the 1960s, none are licenced to tie directly into the series either in the UK or the USA. The games company Bell Toys did produce a now incredibly rare board game based on the series. While copyrighted 1960, this in all probability did not hit the shops until early in 1961. Designed to be played by three to six players, game play revolves around agents trying to carry out acts of sabotage around the world while the player taking the part of 'Danger Man' tries to prevent them.

Tower Press issued a set of four jigsaw puzzles in 1965. All four jigsaws featured illustrations by Walt Howarth and contained approximately 340 pieces, while each of the four puzzles was approximately 17 1/2 inches x 11 3/8 inches in size. The title of the first puzzle was 'The River Chase'. On this first puzzle Drake is shown sat in the back of a police launch as it chases a villain's boat up the River Thames. The second, 'Trouble at the Hotel', shows Drake fighting with two assailants in the lobby of a posh hotel. On the third puzzle,

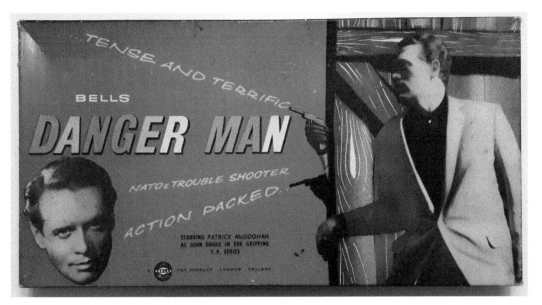

Danger Man board game. (Matt Courtman, www.danger-man.co.uk)

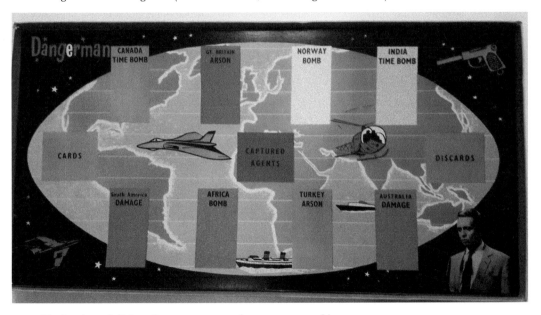

Playing board. (Matt Courtman, www.danger-man.co.uk)

'A Dangerous Moment', Drake is shown at the wheel of his car being pursued both by another vehicle and a low-flying aircraft, while the final jigsaw, 'The Rooftop Adventure', finds Drake hiding in ambush behind a chimney stack. The original cost of these jigsaws was 2s 6d each.

The only other licenced toy for the series was the John Drake Secret Agent Board Game, which was released in the USA by Milton Bradly in 1966. The box artwork shows Drake hitting an armed guard through a plasterwork banister and the artwork is a good likeness of Patrick McGoohan. A small headshot photograph of McGoohan also features on the box lid.

31

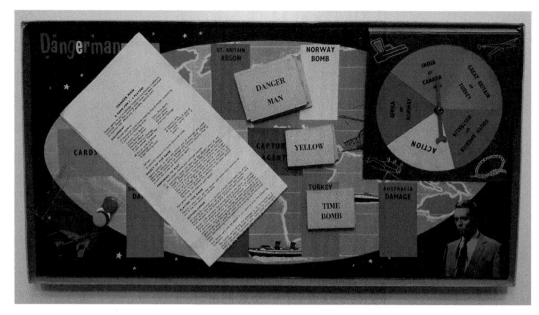

Game contents. (Matt Courtman, www.danger-man.co.uk)

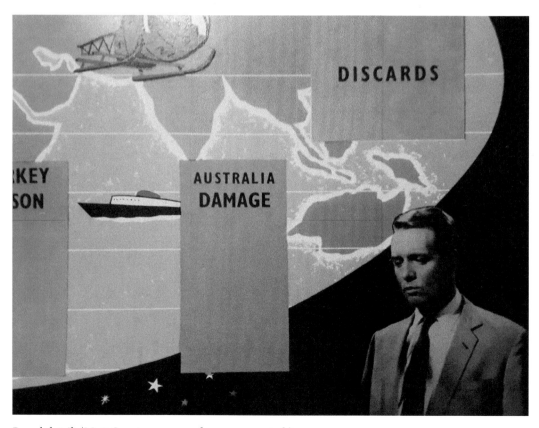

Board detail. (Matt Courtman, www.danger-man.co.uk)

Above: Box detail.
(Matt Courtman,
www.danger-man.co.uk)

Right: Game spinner.
(Matt Courtman,
www.danger-man.co.uk)

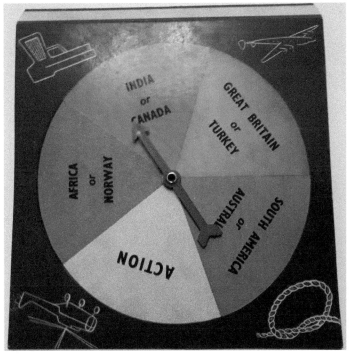

'The River Chase' jigsaw.

'Trouble at the Hotel' jigsaw.

'A Dangerous Moment' jigsaw.

'The Rooftop
Adventure' jigsaw.

Rear of jigsaw
box.

USA edition
Secret Agent game.

Australian edition *Secret Agent* game.

Above left: Box detail comparison.

Above right: Box detail comparison.

The game takes the form of a race between agents to retrieve a briefcase and return it to their headquarters. The game board has painted scenes along each edge, while playing pieces are four coloured target silhouettes, each with a slot so as to retain the small card briefcase also included within the game. Also contained are a die and a deck of cards representing different forms of transport. The game was intended for up to four players. This game was also issued in Australia under licence to John Sands Plc. While essentially the same game, a few minor differences are apparent between the USA issue and the Australian edition, most notably that while the American edition has the games instructions printed within the box lid, the Australian edition features a printed instruction sheet.

Game contents.

Playing
board.

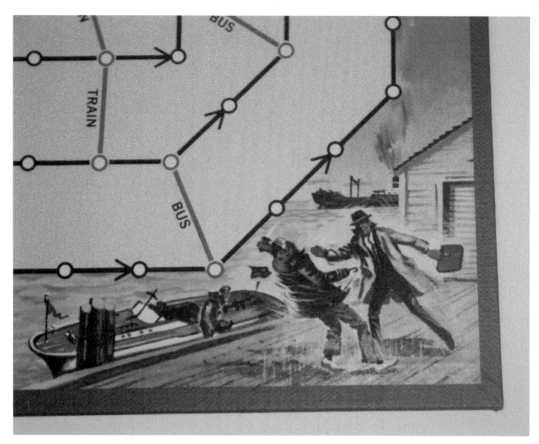

Board detail.

USA instructions.

Comics

Danger Man's first solo comic was produced in the USA in September of 1961 by Dell Publishing. Issued at a price of 15 cents, this comic was issue 1231 in their ongoing series of full colour comics.

This same comic was also released in Spanish for the Mexican and Spanish-speaking markets around the same time.

In Sweden a Swedish version was issued by Centerförlaget in 1962. This same story and artwork would also be serialised over three issues of the Dutch children's magazine *TV2000* during November 1968.

Two further comics were produced in the USA, with the first of them appearing in 1966. The series was now known as *Secret Agent* in America and these two titles, the second of which appeared in 1968, reflected this title change. Both of these new titles were published by Gold Key Comics at a price of 12 cents and were full colour throughout. Issue one from November 1966 featured a story entitled *The Panic Package*, while the second issue published in January of 1968 featured the story *World Wide Woman Hunt*.

In the UK, the first and only solo *Danger Man* comic was published by Thorpe and Porter in 1966. This single-issue British comic was sixty eight pages long and featured four stories, all Illustrated by Mick Anglo, who had also illustrated *The Avengers* comic published by Thorpe and Porter. As with *The Avengers* comic, this saw translated editions being published in several European countries, and like that comic this too was split into two issues for each of those other countries.

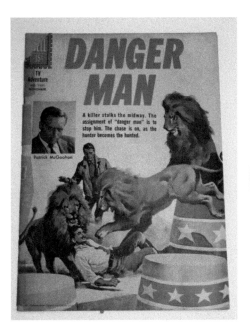 

Above left: Dell *Danger Man* comic.

Above right: Dutch *TV2000*. (Remco Admiraal)

Above left: Secret Agent
Comic No. 1.

Above right: Secret Agent
Comic No. 2.

Left: UK *Danger Man* comic.

In the Netherlands where they were published in 1967, issue one became *John Drake: Onrust in Turkije,* TV classics No. 2101. While issue two was *John Drake: De bewaakte Kapel.* This issue was No. 2104 in the TV classics series of comics.

In Germany where BSV – Williams issued the UK comic as two issues 1967, the first issue became *John Drake: Sarge in Spanien,* with the second issue being *John Drake: Abenteuer in Istanbul.*

Forlaget I.K. (Illustrerede klassikere) were the publisher for the two comics derived from the UK Thorpe and Porter comic in Demark, which were published in 1967. The first of

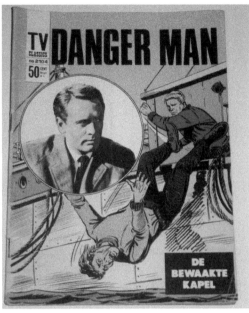

Above left: Dutch comic No. 1.

Above right: Dutch comic No. 2.

Right: German comic No. 1.

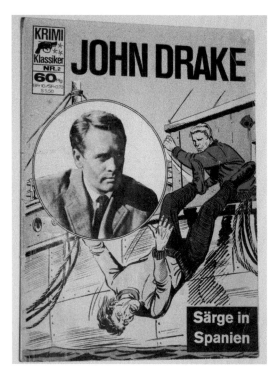

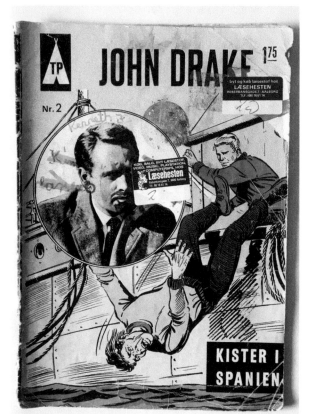

Above left: German comic No. 2.

Above right: Danish comic No. 1.
(Remco Admiraal)

Left: Danish comic No. 2.
(Remco Admiraal)

the two issues was *John Drake: Besvaer I Tyrkiet*, while the second issue was *John Drake: Kister I Spanien.*

In Sweden the Thorpe and Porter comic became *Ett fall for John Drake,* with the first issue being entitled *Trubbel I Turkiet,* while its second issue was *Gravkorets Hemlighet.* These Swedish editions were published by Williams Forlag in 1967.

Over in Spain *Danger Man* became *Agente Secreto* and the publishing company Ferma produced a series of thirty-nine comics or rather *Novelas graficas para adultos* starting in 1966.

 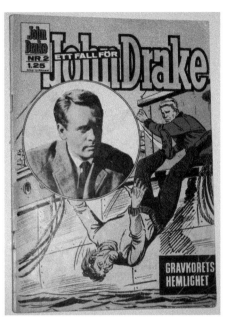

Above left: Swedish comic No. 1.

Above right: Swedish comic No. 2.

Right: Spanish comic.

TV Express comic.

In the UK the first comic book appearance of *Danger Man* was as a weekly text story within the pages of *TV Express*. This children's paper (which also included a strip series based on real wartime exploits as recounted by Col. Pinto of televisions *Spycatcher* series, along with a strip series based on Captain W. E. Johns' *Biggles* books, a TV series that was popular at the time) ran a complete text story in each issue starting in issue 347, in June 1961. This series of stories remained in *TV Express* up until its merger into *TV Comic* in January 1962. In total *Danger Man* would appear in thirty issues of the comic. None of these stories appear to be titled and the only writing credit located is from the last issue he appeared in, where the writer is given as Henry Lewis.

The only other regular comic book appearance in the UK for *Danger Man* wouldn't be for another four years. In 1966 the series was picked up as a strip story in *Lion* comic, upon its merger with *Champion* on 11 June 1966. This strip story would continue for a thirteen-issue run in the combined *Lion* and *Champion* comic, finishing with the 3 September 1966 issue. Artwork for this strip series was by Jesus Blasco, an artist best known for his work on a

Lion and *Champion* comic.

strip in *Valiant* comic, called The Steel Claw. Several of the strips were slightly reworked and republished in 1975 in the *Bumper Story Book for Boys*, appearing under guise of 'Matt Mason Secret Agent'. In the mid-1980s the strips were discovered by comics editor Dez Skinn, who produced mock ups reformatting the strips from the original large British sized pages to the smaller American comic format, with the intentions of producing a graphic novel of these strips for Quality Periodicals, the then owners of what had been Fleetway, *Lion*'s publishers. Sadly this was not to occur.

While it wasn't a regular story or feature, several issues of *Diana*, the girls' comic published by DC Thomson & Co. Ltd, would include items relating to the series during 1966 and 1967. In issue 171, a small image of McGoohan featured alongside similar images of David McCallum, Robert Vaughan and Sean Connery as part of a contest for winning a wristwatch. Of more interest though is issue 173. McGoohan not only features on the cover of this issue, but it also contained an interview with the star. *Diana* also produced a couple of interesting free gifts, in issue 213 a small booklet titled *My Very Own Book of Super Stars* appeared. This small soft cover booklet, described as having 'pages and pages of your favourite stars', featured images of *The Avengers, Danger Man* and a whole host of other television and film stars. Another issues free gift was *Diana's Top Secret Diary*, which again was a small soft covered booklet that included photographs of *The Avengers, The Man from U.N.C.L.E., Danger Man, The Saint,* James Bond, plus others. Various simple codes were also included, which was presented with issue 188.

Left: *Diana* comic.

Below: *Diana's Top Secret Diary*.

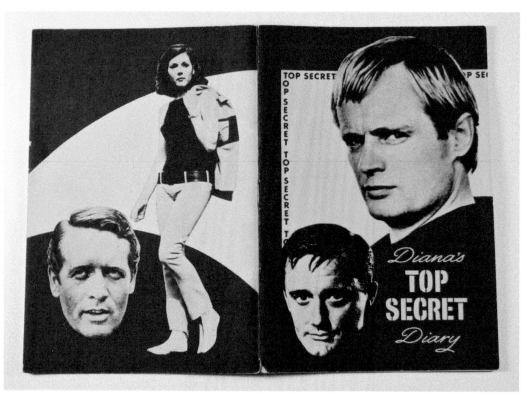

Right: *Diana* comic. (Jaz Wiseman)

Below left: Spy Spot from *TV Tornado* No. 4.

Below right: McGoohan quiz from *TV Tornado* No. 32.

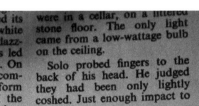

Left: *Thierry La Fronde* comic.

Below: *Thierry La Fronde* comic with *Danger Man* content.

Above left: *Destination Danger* comic.

Above right: *Destination Danger* bound editions. (Bernard Dunne)

While not a regular feature or story, mention of *Danger Man* could quite often be found in *TV Tornado* comic. While most instances were just passing mentions or images, a couple of issues had slightly more. Issue 4 had a very small piece on spy equipment, while issue 32 had a small quiz on McGoohan.

Before becoming its own title, *Destination Danger,* as the show was known in France, started as a support strip in *Thierry La Fronde* comic books in 1964. *Thierry La Fronde* was a popular French television series at the time, being their equivalent of the British Robin Hood. Set at the time of the Hundred Years' War, Thierry is a young noble man turned outlaw fighting against the tyranny of the English occupation. Some issues of this French comic were bound into larger editions containing several issues of the comic. Strangely there is at least one issue of the comic, issue 22, which does not actually contain John Drake.

Magazines

Danger Man seems to have been particularly popular in Germany, where a very long running magazine was published, starting in 1963. *John Drake* magazine would run for 464 issues and into the early 1980s, publishing a complete John Drake adventure in every issue, although random photographs from completely unrelated television shows or films would quite often appear on the cover. This publication was produced by Wolfgang Marken Verlog Gmbh. Issues of this magazine were occasionally bound into larger volumes containing several consecutive issues, with a new photo cover surrounding them. Some issues found their way to the newsstands having been bound into collections with other unrelated titles from the same publisher.

The Spanish publishers Ediciones Este in 1964, as issue 14 in their *Figuras de la T.V. – Biografia lustrada* series, produced *Patrick Mac Goohan* [sic] *Agente Secreto.*

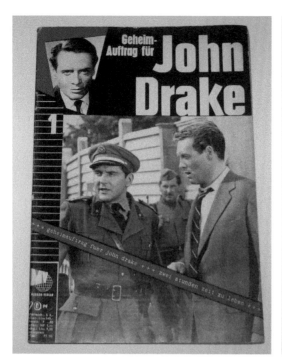 

Above left: First issue of German *John Drake* magazine.

Above right: Spanish magazine. (Bernard Dunne)

Some very late issues of *John Drake* magazine.

TV Listings Magazines

As is often the case with television series, many other unrelated magazines would also, as part of their editorial, include pieces on the series. The following are just a few of these many such occurrences. The film magazine *Showtime*, published by Rank Theatre Division Ltd, was one such magazine. In their September 1965 issue, it included an interview with McGoohan under the title 'If Bond Came Up Against – Danger Man'.

The main magazines to include features have to be the vintage *TV Times* and other listings magazines from around the world. It has to be mentioned here that during the 1960s the *TV Times* did not cover every region of the UK, as several regions had their own equivalents to the magazine. In the Midlands it was *TV World,* published by Odhams Press, which as well as the regular listings also contained in August 1965 a *Danger Man* story entitled 'Shark Bait' written by Robert Holmes, which ran over several issues.

The Viewer was the listings magazine for both Scottish Television and Tyne Tees Television. This magazine, on its 28 November 1965 dated issue, would feature both a cover and a behind the scenes feature on the series. While in the Westward region, *Look Westward* was that region's own listings magazine, in which the series featured on the cover of 3 October 1965 edition with a feature entitled 'Hat's – But no swelled head'.

The main ITV magazine at the time was still the *TV Times*, which covered by far the largest amount of UK television regions. Several issues of this magazine are notable for containing features relating to *Danger Man*, starting with the 11–17 September 1960 edition, which contained a feature introducing the first episode along with the listing for

TV World.

Left: *Look Westward*. (Matt Courtman, www.danger-man.co.uk)

Below: *TV Times*. (Matt Courtman, www.danger-man.co.uk)

such. Other notable issues to contain features are the 10–16 October 1964 issue, which had a feature entitled 'Dicing with Danger Man'. Then a few weeks later in the 31 October–6 November 1964 issue there was another feature: 'Cobra in my Pocket'.

The 2–8 January 1965 edition had a full colour cover for the series but did not include a feature. Once again, the 18–24 September 1965 issue featured McGoohan on the cover but

Above left: *TV Week* (Australia, Victoria edition). (Matt Courtman, www.danger-man.co.uk)

Above right: *TV Weekly New Zealand*. (Matt Courtman, www.danger-man.co.uk)

no feature. The following three weeks issues, 25 September–1 October 1965, 2–8 October 1965 and 9–15 October 1965, did, however, contain a three part feature on McGoohan and *Danger Man*. These were entitled 'McGoohan magic, in and out of Danger Man', More McGoohan magic: He's a home and family man', and 'More McGoohan magic: Scared... of having nothing to do' respectively.

Another interesting article appeared in the 2–8 September 1967 issue. Written by George Markstein, the feature 'When the danger was real' recounts several incidents that took place during the filming of various episodes, most notably 'Not so Jolly Roger', which was filmed on Redsands Fort, situated in the Thames estuary, which at the time was home to a pirate radio station.

In Australia the listings magazine was *TV Week*, which was produced in several regional variations. These are issues known to be of interest to *Danger Man* fans, but there are quite probably other issues to have contained material of interest. In the Sidney region both the 13 February 1965 and 27 March 1965 editions would both carry features on *Danger Man*. These were titled 'It's that Danger Man again' and 'Danger Man at work' respectively.

In *TV Week*'s Victoria edition *Danger Man* appeared upon the front cover with a feature 'Danger! He's a man of Action' on 13 November 1965.

Then there are several known issues of the New South Wales edition of *TV Week*. 19 February 1966 contained the first part of a two-part feature entitled 'That Man McGoohan', the second part appearing the following week on 26 February 1966. 7 May

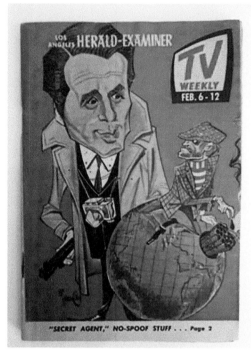

Above left: *Chicago Tribune TV Week*. (Matt Courtman, www.danger-man.co.uk)

Above right: *LA Herald Examiner TV Weekly*. (Matt Courtman, www.danger-man.co.uk)

1966 would see another feature, 'That dashing Danger Man' and later that year on 30 July 1966 the article 'McGoohan out of Danger – now enter the Baron' appeared, which is more about the new series *The Baron* replacing it in the schedules than it is about *Danger Man*.

TV Weekly in New Zealand covered the series on 1 August 1966 with both a cover and accompanying feature 'Danger Man Dies in London – But McGoohan lives on...'. Then again on 22 May 1967 there was an article entitled 'The Day they knocked out "Danger Man"'.

As in the UK several different listings magazines existed around the USA, which would include pieces on *Secret Agent*, as it was known there. In the *Chicago Tribune TV Week* on 10 July 1965 an article 'Imported Adventure', referring to the series arrival in the USA, appeared along with an accompanying cover. Another American TV listings magazine, *LA Herald-Examiner TV Weekly,* 6 February 1966, featured the star on its cover with no accompanying feature, just a listing for *Secret Agent*'s broadcasting that week. The best known of the American listings magazines, *TV Guide*, included a feature on McGoohan in their 14 May 1966 issue entitled 'James Bond is no hero to him'.

In France McGoohan appeared on the cover of at least two listings magazines: *Tele Programme Magazine* on 16–22 July 1961 and *Tele 7 Jours* on 21–27 September 1963.

Other Magazine

Magazines other than just the TV listings guides would also often feature articles on the series. The film magazine *Photoplay* featured it in an April 1961 article, 'Who'd be a TV

The Weekly News. (Matt Courtman, www.danger-man.co.uk)

hero – Why Danger Man scared me'. In August 1961, *Danger Man* was included in the article 'Don't blame us for teenage violence'. The May 1965 issue included the feature 'TV's mystery Danger man', while in November 1965 there was an article entitled 'It's fun being a TV hero'.

Over consecutive issues from 9 October to 30 October 1965 *Woman* magazine included the four-part feature Dossier on *Danger Man.*

Everybody's, a UK gossip type magazine, included an article on McGoohan: 'This broth of a boy is always in a stew'.

In their 2 April 1966 issue *Trend and Boyfriend* included a small feature on McGoohan: 'The bird-shy Danger man!'

Spies, Spoofs & Super Guys, published by Dell in the USA in 1966, concentrated on all things spy related and hiding among its contents was a feature entitled 'Dossier on Drake'. This magazine is actually quite a treasure trove for those with an interest in 1960s television and movie spies, also containing features on James Bond, Derick Flint, Harry Palmer, *I Spy*, Matt Helm, *Get Smart* and the *Man from U.N.C.L.E.*

During 1965 *The Weekly News*, a British weekly newspaper published by DC Thomson, ran a series of *Danger Man* stories over several weeks, even featuring the show on the papers cover in May of that year.

Records

Singles

Always a collector's favourite for any television show is the theme music from the series, and with *Danger Man* there are three distinctly different themes. The original theme for

Red Price Combo single.

Ivor Slaney Orchestra single

Edwin Astley single.

the series in the UK was composed by Edwin Astley and issued in the UK by the Red Price Combo on the Parlophone label. R4789 being issued in 1961 as 'Theme from Danger Man' with the b side being an unrelated track called 'Blackjack', this version was the main theme as used on the first series of the show.

When the series returned as hour-long episodes a second version of the theme was created by Edwin Astley. This version was called 'High Wire', and the Ivor Slaney Orchestra would release a cover version of Astley's 'High Wire' theme on HMV POP 1347 in 1964. 'Sacramento' was the unrelated b side of this UK release.

Another cover version of 'High Wire' appeared on the Pye label in 1964 (Pye 7N 15700). This UK issued single performed by the Bob Leaper Orchestra had an unrelated b side entitled 'The Lost World'.

Edwin Astley released his own version of 'High Wire' as 'Danger Man' in 1965 in the UK. This version was the main theme as used in the second, third and fourth season of the show. Released on RCA Victor (RCA 1492) the *Danger Man* theme was backed by another Astley composed theme, that of *The Saint*. This single was previously issued in New Zealand in 1964 as 'High Wire' (theme from *Danger Man*) and *The Saint* on RCA Victor 60409.

The other distinct theme for the show was the specially composed title song for the shows American release 'Secret Agent Man'. The original version and that used on the show was recorded by the singer Johnny Rivers. In the UK this theme was released in 1966 on the Liberty label (LIB 12023), with the b side 'Tom Dooley'.

It appeared also in Australia in 1966, with 'You Dig' being the reverse. This was once again on Liberty (LIB 66159).

Johnny Rivers' version appeared in Italy, again with a different b side, this time 'Green, Green'. This 1966 release was on Liberty LIB 12027.

The Johnny Rivers release of the theme in Brazil was backed by yet another different b side: 'The Snake'. This was also issued on a different record label RCA Victor (FC-55016). Once again this release was in 1966.

Johnny Rivers UK single.

Left: Hal Blaine single.

Below left: Japanese Clee-shays single front. (Bernard Dunne)

Below right: Japanese Clee-shays single reverse. (Bernard Dunne)

The American group The Ventures released a cover version of 'Secret Agent Man', with a James Bond-related b side in 1966. In the UK this was on the Liberty label (LIB 316).

'Secret Agent Man' was covered on the Dunhill label in the USA by Hal Blaine with the b side track being 'The Invaders' in 1967 (Dunhill D4102).

In Japan the Clee-shays put out two singles on the Union label. The first featured a track called 'John Drake', which was a slight reworking of the Astley *Danger Man* theme, with a b side called 'Drum beat', which was on Union US-164 and issued in 1967. Their second single featured a cover version of 'Secret Agent Man', with the other side being their rendition of the *Batman* theme. It was released in 1967 on Union US-504.

Now while not directly released in connection with the series, it is worth adding here that the single 'Mio Amore Sta Lontano' was performed by Angelique and released in 1966 on the Pye label (7N 17066). This song, originally written and recorded by the English pop group The Zombies, was featured in several of the hour-long episodes of *Danger Man*.

Bruce Willis single.

One other single worth mentioning here is Bruce Willis' release on Motown (ZB41437) in 1987:

'Secret Agent Man James Bond is Back', which was mashup of 'Secret Agent Man' and James Bond music.

Many of the records mentioned here saw releases around the world, in some cases on different record labels, occasionally with picture sleeves. There were just too many for space to allow.

EPs

In Japan several extended playing records featured cover versions of 'Secret Agent Man'. The Ventures put two EPs on the Liberty label: the first 'Secret Agent Men' on Liberty LEP 2250 in 1966 and the second on Liberty LP-4170 in 1967, which contained 'Secret Agent

Above left: Ventures EP, Japan.

Above right: Clee-shays EP, Japan.

Man', 'Man from U.N.C.L.E.', 'The Batman Theme' and '007'.

The Clee-shays also put out an EP in Japan, which was on Union SUW-30 in 1967. Their EP contained the tracks 'Secret Agent Man', 'I spy', 'John Drake' and 'Thrush theme' (from *The Man from U.N.C.L.E.*).

Albums

An album of *Music from the TV series Secret Agent* was released in the USA on RCA victor LPM-3630 (Mono) or LSP-3630 (Stereo) in 1966.

RCA Victor also issued the album *Secret Agent Meets the Saint*. This 1965 album featured Edwin Astley tracks that were then used on the *Secret Agent* album as well as tracks from another British TV series, *The Saint*. Once again available in either mono (LPM 3467) or stereo (LSP 3467).

The HMV released *Your Favourite TV and Radio Themes* (HMV CLP1565) from 1962 contains the Red Price Combo version of the *Danger Man* theme. A later album in this series from HMV (volume 5) apparently contains 'High Wire' by Ivor Slaney Orchestra.

Secret Agent LP.

Secret Agent meets The Saint LP.

Above left: *Your Favourite TV and Radio Themes* LP.

Above right: *Top TV Themes* LP.

Above left: Reverse of Japanese Clee-shays LP. (Bernard Dunne)

Above right: Ventures 1979 Japanese reissue. (Bernard Dunne)

The James Wright and his Orchestra album *Top TV Themes*, released by Embassy (WLP 6076) in 1965, includes a recording of 'High Wire'.

The album *Sounds for Spies and Private Eyes*, released on United Artists (ULP/SULP 1115) in 1966, contains a version of *Secret Agent Man* by Al Caiola.

Time for TV, by Brian Fahey and his Orchestra and released by Columbia Studio 2 (Stereo TWO 175), was released in 1967. This LP contains a cover version of the *Danger Man* theme along with renditions of *The Avengers, The Baron, The Man from U.N.C.L.E., The Saint* and *Thunderbirds*. This UK issued LP has a very nice picture sleeve showing *The Avengers*.

61

Action TV and Movie Pictures' Themes: Theme from the Man from U.N.C.L.E was released by Union (UPS 5091) in Japan in 1967 by the Clee-shays. This album features a photograph of John Drake on the reverse of the record sleeve, with both 'Secret Agent Man' and the track 'John Drake' appearing on the album.

The self-titled album *The Ventures* saw the group covering several TV themes including 'Secret Agent Man'. This was originally released in America in 1966 on the Dolton Records label (BLP-2042), being reissued on the United Artists label in 1979 (GXH-41). This reissue also saw release in Japan in the same year.

Trading Cards

Another popular area of collecting is trading cards and, in the UK, the firm Somportex would issue a set of cards with bubble gum in 1966. This set of seventy-two cards each had a black and white photograph from the series on the front, while a story is told on the back of the cards, when read in the correct order. Cards are approximately 57 mm x 78 mm in size. A special *Danger Man* offer was also made on the back of the cards, stating that if twenty-four wrappers were sent to Somportex you would receive your free personalised identity bracelet.

In Spain the firm Fher S. A. issued a set of 162 stickers in 1966, which were accompanied by an album for you to place your collection in.

While these are the only two actual *Danger Man* sets of cards that are known about, images of McGoohan and *Danger Man* did make it into other larger sets featuring multiple shows or actors. A&BC gum issued a set of seventy cards called 'Who-z-at star in 1961. Because of the way these cards work, McGoohan appears on two cards in this set. Card 18 is the main card to feature him, with a colourised, slightly drawn over photograph appearing on the front of the card, while half of the reverse is taken up with a brief biography. The other half of the cards reverse is a small photograph and question relating to a different card in the set. The second card to feature McGoohan is card 44. The main personality

Somportex wrapper.

Above: Somportex cards.

Right: Album for Spanish sticker set.
(Remco Admiraal)

Who-Z-at Star 18.

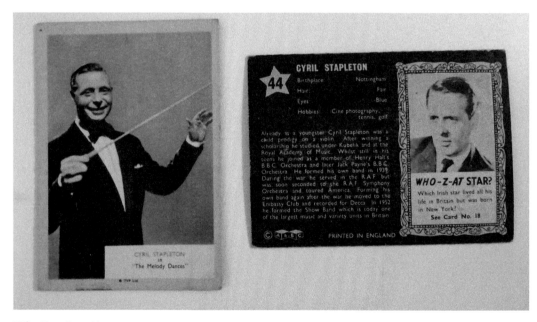

Who-Z-at Star 44.

on this card is Cyril Stapleton, but the rear of the card has a small photograph relating to McGoohan, card 18.

Another set of cards issued by A&BC gum in 1961 was the 'Fotostars' set. Each card in this forty-card set was sectioned into three, each third of the card showing a photograph of a different star. The back, also sectioned into thirds, had a short biography of each star.

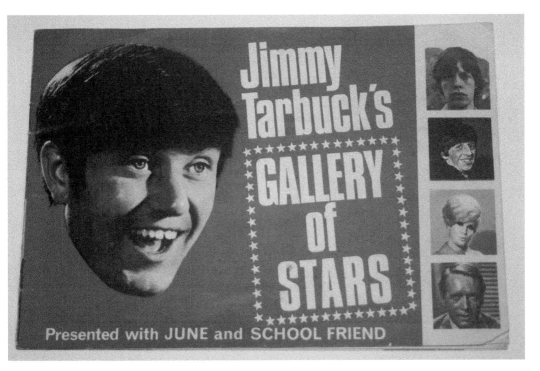

Jimmy Tarbuck's *Gallery of Stars* album.

Mister
Softee
card.

ABC Minors card.

Victoria biscuits card.

The cards are not numbered, but Patrick McGoohan appears alongside Bruce Forsyth and Hughie Green.

Jimmy Tarbuck's Gallery of Stars was actually a small booklet given away in an issue of *June and School Friend* during the mid-1960s. It was an album for you to put a collection of small cut out pictures of various stars, which were being given away each week in the comic. McGoohan features on the front of the album as well as being card 101 in the set.

A set of twenty-five cards was produced by Mister Softee ice cream in 1962, entitled 'TV Personalities'. Patrick McGoohan appears on card 4 in the series. The cards image of him is another of those strangely over drawn photographs reminiscent of the Bromoil style of photography, a process where the original image is over drawn and the photograph bleached out leaving just the illustration.

Another set to use this style of card and the same image, but on a different colour background, was the third series of ABC Minors cards, once again issued around 1962. McGoohan appeared on card 3 of this set. To collect these cards you would need to attend the ABC Minors Club each week, almost like an attendance card. Each week a different card would be given out until, after several weeks, depending on your attendance, you would have collected the full set.

The company Victoria issued at least one card featuring Patrick McGoohan as John Drake in a set of cards that were issued with chocolate biscuits in Belgium.

Promotional and Miscellaneous Items

In both France and Spain postcards were issued for the show, while matchbox labels featuring *Danger Man* appeared in the Netherlands. Strangely in France a pair of *Destination Danger* socks appeared.

Sheet music appeared for 'High Wire', published by Robbins Music Corp. Ltd in 1965. This was available either as an individual sheet for just that theme at 2s 6d, or in a

Matchbox label.

Robbins Top TV Themes.

compilation book of sheet music *Robbins Top TV Themes*, which contained several themes, including both 'High Wire' and 'The Saint', at a cost of 5*s*.

In the USA two different editions of the sheet music for the American theme 'Secret Agent Man' were published. The first and probably more desirable edition featured a photo cover of McGoohan in the role of John Drake, while the other edition shows the group The Ventures who had recorded a version of the song. Both editions of this were published by Trousdale Music Publications at a publish price of 75 cents.

What is considered to be the fourth series of *Danger Man* was two final colour episodes produced in 1966 and broadcast in February 1967. These final two episodes were combined

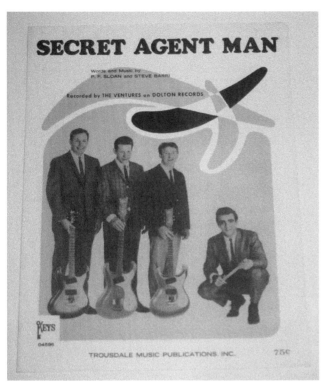

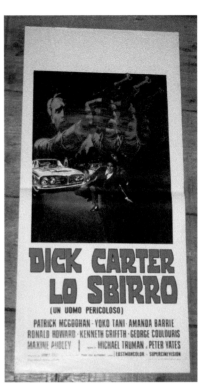

Above left: 'Secret Agent Man' sheet music.

Above right: Italian poster.

Right: Italian poster

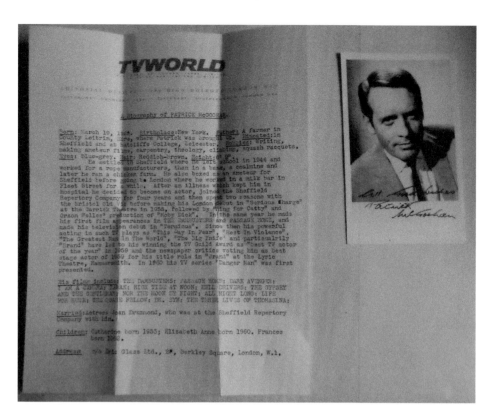

Above: Studio fan card and letter sent out by *TV World* magazine. (Bernard Dunne)

Left: Postcard with printed signature.

and reedited into a feature film *Koroshi,* which saw release in several countries including Italy, Germany and Japan.

As is often the case with many TV shows, fans of the series would write into the studio requesting autographs. Studios would quite often produce fan cards, which were postcard sized photographs with a pre-printed signature that would be sent out to those having requested such. Originals of these cards are highly sought after and over the years have been reproduced by *Prisoner* fan clubs.

The Prisoner

The Prisoner is one of those sixties enigmas, a series that just won't go away. It has a following equalled by few others; every atom of its meaning has been analysed and investigated, from every possible and conceivable angle. Where is the village? Who is No. 6? Who is No. 1? Apparently even a psychology course has used the series as a basis. The purpose of this book, however, is not to delve into all of the critical analysis of the series, but to investigate the collectibles that have appeared as a result of the show. So this is it in a nutshell, no annulus, just the basics. An unnamed secret agent resigns. He is then abducted and taken to the village. No one has a name, only a number. He is No. 6. The villages' location is unknown and is presided over by No. 2. Is there a No. 1? Any attempts to leave or escape the village are stopped by the mysterious rovers, giant balloon-like creatures. 'I am not a number, I am a free man'. The following episodes concerned No. 6's various escape attempts, and his desire to discover more about his captors and surroundings.

The series was made in the hour-long format, with seventeen episodes being produced. It was created by the series star Patrick McGoohan, though the script editor George Markstein should also be credited for his contribution. Much speculation has always been made as to the identity of No. 6. Many including George Markstein maintain that he was John Drake, the character McGoohan had played in *Danger Man*, though McGoohan himself always denied this (I personally believe No. 6 was John Drake). Arguments like this are pointless in reality. The official line always has to be that John Drake and No. 6 are not the same person, for the very simple reason that if it were to be officially acknowledged that this was the case, Ralph Smart as the creator of *Danger Man* and John Drake would be due royalties for the use of his character within another series.

Ultimately the series was made as entertainment, and it should be regarded as such. Confusing it may be, and it may challenge ways of thinking and even bring up psychological questions, but don't lose sight of its entertainment value.

Over the years many books have been written, putting forward different critiques about *The Prisoner*. For the most part these studies of the series and its history have been omitted. This book is more interested in the novels and other products that have appeared. Also for the most part attempts have been made to remain with products contemporary to the shows original broadcasts, though a few exceptions have been made.

'Be seeing you!'

Books

Surprisingly at the time of the shows broadcast in the UK, no books relating to the series were produced. However, over in the USA three paperback novels would appear. Ace Books were the publishers and they started with *The Prisoner* by Thomas M. Disch, published in 1969. This particular novel has apparently always led to a lot of debate among

Above left: USA paperback 1.

Above right: USA paperback 2.

Right: USA paperback 3.

Above left: UK hardback 1.

Above right: UK hardback 2.

Prisoner fans as to how much of it is actually based upon the series and how much is Dischs' own view of society at that time. Also published in 1969 was *The Prisoner: Number Two* by David McDaniel, a name well known to genre fans as he also penned several of the *Man from U.N.C.L.E.* series of novels. The final title in the series *The Prisoner: A Day in the Life* by Hank Stine was published in 1970. All three of these titles has full colour photographic covers.

The three Ace Books paperbacks would eventually see publication in the UK in 1979 when both *The Prisoner* by Thomas M. Disch and *The Prisoner: A Day in the Life* by Hank Stine were published in hardback editions by Dobson Books Ltd. Paperback editions followed, published by New English Library (NEL paperbacks), with *The Prisoner* by Thomas M. Disch, now also subtitled 'I am not a number. I am a free man', coming out in 1980. *The Prisoner: A Day in the Life* By Hank Stine appeared in 1981. Then finally what had been the second of the USA series, *The Prisoner: Number Two*, was published under its new British title *The Prisoner: Who Is Number Two?* by David McDaniel as the third of the UK publications in 1982.

The Thomas M. Disch novel *The Prisoner* saw two different editions being published in Japan by Hayakawa Shobo. Publication dates on these are unclear, but the earlier of the two editions appears to show a 'Rover' rising up out of the water, while the rear cover is an image of the cover from its USA publication. The later edition has a cover replicating a jigsaw puzzle.

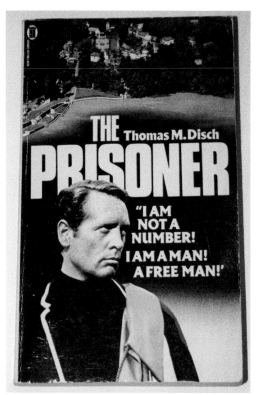

Above left: UK paperback 1.

Above right: UK paperback 2.

Left: UK paperback 3.

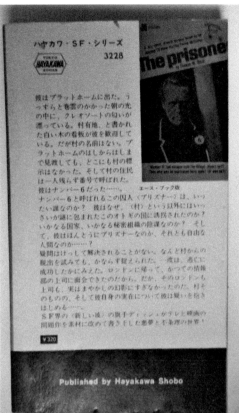

Above left: Japanese paperback first style.
(Bernard Dunne)

Above right: Japanese paperback first style
rear cover. (Bernard Dunne)

Right: Japanese paperback second style.
(Bernard Dunne)

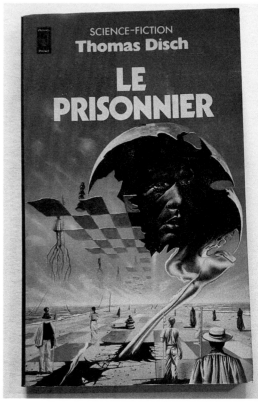

Above left: Israeli paperback. (Jaz Wiseman)

Above right: French paperback.
(© Rick Davy, www.theunmutual.co.uk)

Left: French paperback. (© Rick Davy,
www.theunmutual.co.uk)

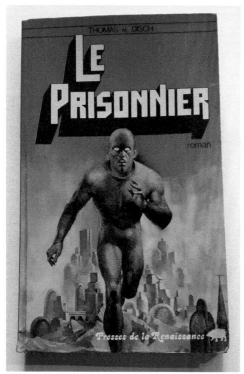

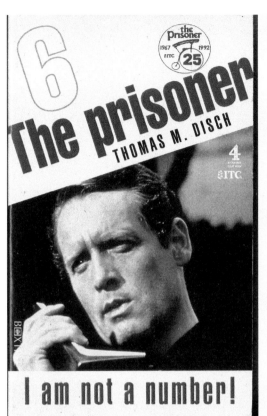
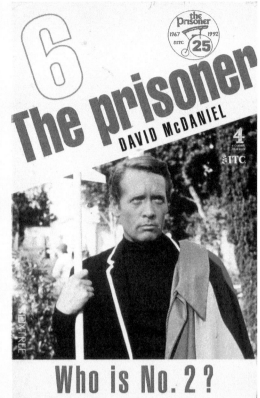

Above: 1992 Boxtree releases.
(© Rick Davy, www.theunmutual.co.uk)

Right: 2009 edition of *The Prisoner* paperback.

The David McDaniel novel *The Prisoner: Number Two* would also see publication in Israel.

In France two different editions of Thomas M. Dischs' *The Prisoner* were published in 1977 by Presses de la Renaissance. The reason why they released it with two different cover designs in the same year is unknown. One also has to wonder on the choice of cover, as while one is quite evocative of the series in a surrealist type of style, the other gives a much more science fiction type futuristic flavour, which does not really reflect the series.

In 1992, two of the novels, *The Prisoner* by Thomas M. Disch and *The Prisoner: Who Is Number Two?* by David McDaniel saw publication by Boxtree Books to coincide with the Channel 4 showing of the series in the UK at that time.

All three of *The Prisoner* novels were gathered together into an omnibus edition that saw publication in the UK by Carlton in 2002. Then, with the advent of *The Prisoner* being remade in 2009, Penguin Books republished the Thomas M. Disch novel, complete with an image of Sir Ian McKellan, the new No. 2, on its cover, tying it into the new series.

While several different generic television related annuals featured both McGoohan and *Danger Man*, the only direct reference to *The Prisoner* thus located is in the Purnell

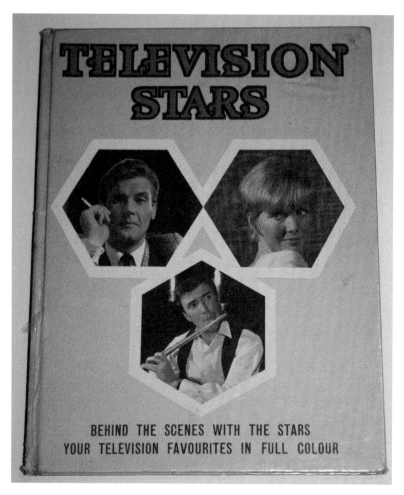

Television Stars Book.

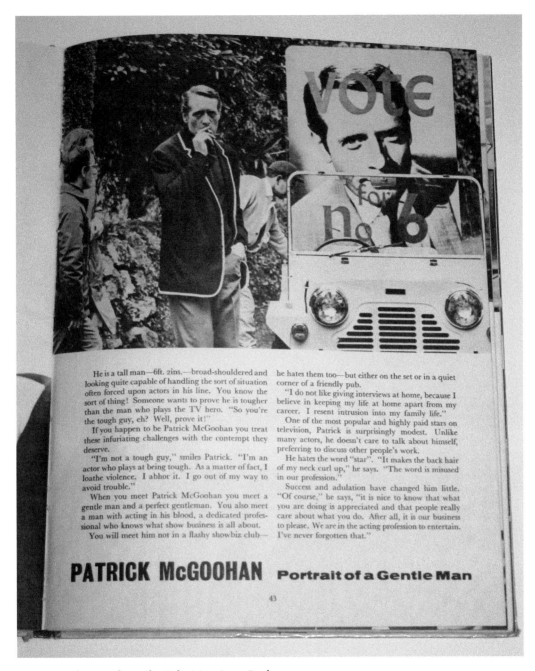

He is a tall man—6ft. 2ins.—broad-shouldered and looking quite capable of handling the sort of situation often forced upon actors in his line. You know the sort of thing! Someone wants to prove he is tougher than the man who plays the TV hero. "So you're the tough guy, eh? Well, prove it!"

If you happen to be Patrick McGoohan you treat these infuriating challenges with the contempt they deserve.

"I'm not a tough guy," smiles Patrick. "I'm an actor who plays at being tough. As a matter of fact, I loathe violence. I abhor it. I go out of my way to avoid trouble."

When you meet Patrick McGoohan you meet a gentle man and a perfect gentleman. You also meet a man with acting in his blood, a dedicated professional who knows what show business is all about. You will meet him not in a flashy showbiz club—

he hates them too—but either on the set or in a quiet corner of a friendly pub.

"I do not like giving interviews at home, because I believe in keeping my life at home apart from my career. I resent intrusion into my family life."

One of the most popular and highly paid stars on television, Patrick is surprisingly modest. Unlike many actors, he doesn't care to talk about himself, preferring to discuss other people's work.

He hates the word "star". "It makes the back hair of my neck curl up," he says. "The word is misused in our profession."

Success and adulation have changed him little. "Of course," he says, "it is nice to know that what you are doing is appreciated and that people really care about what you do. After all, it is our business to please. We are in the acting profession to entertain. I've never forgotten that."

PATRICK McGOOHAN Portrait of a Gentle Man

43

An inside page from the *Television Stars Book*.

Television Stars Book (*c.* 1967, no year given in book). This annual sized book has a feature and photographs of McGoohan filming his new show, *The Prisoner*, entitled 'Patrick McGoohan Portrait of a Gentle Man'. The cover of this book is pale blue with three hexagonal photographs on the cover showing Roger Moore, Petula Clark and Roy Castle, while the spine is a dark mauvish pink.

Next to no toys were produced for *The Prisoner*, and this story recounted to Martin Gainsford several years ago by Richard Culley goes some way as to explaining the reason for this.

Richard Culley was a senior executive at AP Merchandising, which was to become Century 21, having previously worked on merchandising of things as diverse as *Batman* and the Daleks. AP Merchandising was the company that handled much of the licencing and merchandise relating to various ITC properties, most predominantly the Gerry Anderson series. Richard, a senior executive with them, was given the job of meeting with Patrick McGoohan, at Borehamwood, to discuss the possible licencing of *The Prisoner* on products.

Richard was apparently quite nervous of this meeting as he had heard of McGoohan's sometimes fiery temperament. After he had waited a few hours he was eventually ushered in to see McGoohan, during what was quite likely a lunch break during filming. There was McGoohan, cup of tea and a sandwich in hand, answering questions of various production people popping into see him. Richard quickly realised that McGoohan was not a man of great patience, especially with seemingly trivial stuff like merchandise. Richard nervously presented McGoohan with some artwork and various ideas of how to present *The Prisoner* to younger readers as a comic strip (most likely for *TV21 or TV Tornado* comic). McGoohan gave them a quick glance but no more, Richard then handed him a mock-up No. 6 doll. (Quite probably an Action Man or Tommy Gunn doll. Pedigree would produce the *Captain Scarlet* doll, Tommy Gunn was their own version of a 12 inch tall fighting soldier figure.) McGoohan handled it, sneered, threw the figure back across the desk, then in very Prisoner like tones declared, 'I will not be a dolly or a comic strip. Goodbye!'.

Dinky Toys Mini Moke showing black windscreen surround and unpainted sides. (Vectis)

Dinky Toys Mini Moke showing silver windscreen surround and painted sides.

Dinky Toys catalogue No. 4.

From this meeting it would seems suprising that any products for the series were indeed licenced. One that was, however, possibly because McGoohan's likeness was not required, was The Prisoner Mini Moke, Dinky Toys model No. 106 produced in 1968. Dinky already had a Mini Moke in their range, well actually two, a civilian version, Dinky Toys No. 342, and a military version (Dinky Toys No. 601), the latter coming with parachute and sledge. So it was

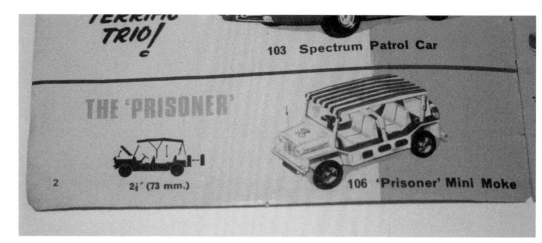

TR10!

103 Spectrum Patrol Car

THE 'PRISONER'

2   2⅞" (73 mm.)

106 'Prisoner' Mini Moke

Dinky Toys catalogue No 5.

Moke wheel comparison.

a simple job for them to convert the existing version and issue a model of the village taxi. The Dinky Toys model is around 73 mm in length and painted white, with a sticker depicting the 'penny farthing' bicycle upon the bonnet. This opens to enable the models engine to be seen. A removable spare tyre is attached to the rear of the vehicle. The windscreen surround is pressed out from a thin sheet of metal, while it has a black plastic steering wheel and a small white plastic aerial at the front. Its white plastic canopy has red and white stripes running front to back across its top. The model also has tan-coloured running boards and 'taxi' printed on the number plates. The original price for the model in 1968 was 6s 9d.

Several minor variations of this model have been noted. The main variations, firstly, are the pressed metal window surround on some models is a base silver metal, while on other versions the window surround is black.

Mini Moke headlights comparison. (Brian Nightingale)

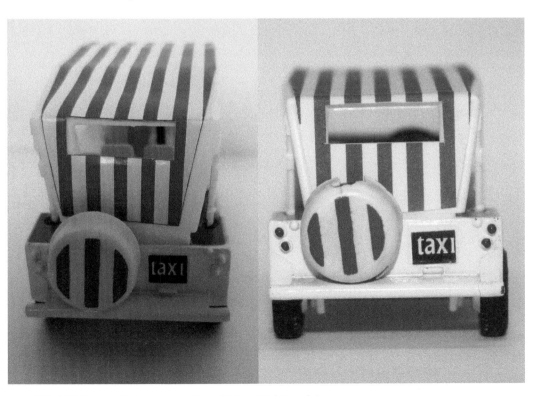

Mini Moke rear lights comparison. (Brian Nightingale)

Above: Mini Moke engine comparison.

Left: Mini Moke axel comparison.

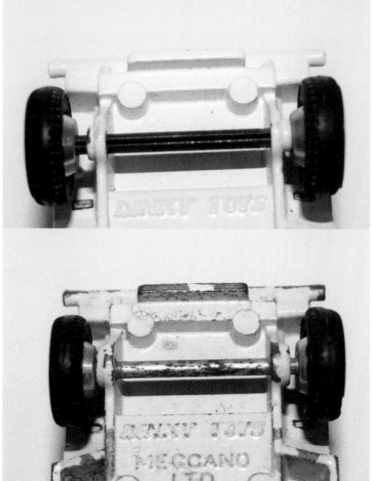

TV Century 21 advert for Mini Moke.

The second variation concerns the wheels. Some are spun metal and the axle sticks through the middle of the wheel with the tip of it is visible, while on others the axles tip is fully encased within a solid cast wheel.

The third place on the model to look at is the area just below the running board on the side. On some versions the middle of the raised area is painted tan, while on others this has been left white.

Fourthly on some versions of the model the lights and grill have not been painted – normally the grill and front lights are silver with the rear lights painted red.

The fifth and sixth variations to note only come to light on a more detailed inspection of the model. The fifth item to differ from model to model is the engine, which is only noticed by opening the bonnet. On some models the engine is white while on others it has been painted gold.

The sixth and last difference of note between models concerns the axles: most models have a solid axle, but some appear to have a split axle.

Several variations of these different details have been noticed during the research for this book. For example, one has solid wheels with silver windscreen and tan side panels, while another had solid wheels with a silver windscreen but white side panels. Yet another version had visible axle tips with a black windscreen and tan side panels. Given the scarcity of this model, it is not really possible to judge which versions of this are the rarest, but it is not uncommon for these sorts of changes to occur during the production run of a toy.

Comics

Unlike *Danger Man*, *The Prisoner* never had a weekly story in any comic book at the time of its original broadcasts. While it didn't appear as story in its own right, it did crop up in a couple of comics. The most well-known occurrence of this is issue 48 of *TV Tornado* from City Magazines. This issue cover, dated 9 December 1967, has a full painting of McGoohan

TV Tornado issue 48.

Napoleon and Illya will be

COVER MAN

THE PRISONER—
as played by Patrick
McGoohan in the series
of that name.

their
trudg
to th
pack
an he
back

ROG
Th
hotel
Und
shou
trick
child
want
sittir
ing
mov
old
hom
and
it's
who
the
eat
the
B
Cai

blocks of that enormous monu-
ment until they were three-
parts up, when they rested to

Right: *TV Tornado* issue 48 contents.

Below: *TV Tornado* Star Spot from issue 15.

Here is the first of a series
of badges we'll be running
during the next few weeks—
that of the 17th Lancers,
raised in 1773.

s if you're
nd it's prefer-
ave O levels—
ve a four-year
hip for In-
British Photo-
exams.
vely, you can
years full-time
ool.

**Sean
Caffrey**

Yard is back in
a new assistant,

ondon. He's 6 ft.
f Arts. He likes
oking and is a

STAR★SPOT

YOU know Patrick McGoohan
as *Danger Man* John Drake.
For that's the part he played
through several series (and the
programmes are still being
repeated on TV).

But for the last year, Pat
has been busy at the studios on
a new adventure series with a
secret agent background. It's
called *The Prisoner*.

Expect to see it in autumn.

ORM'S POSTBAG

87

Smash comic 109.

as the Prisoner. Disappointingly, inside there is just the smallest of photographs and a single sentence about him. A few other issues are worth mentioning: issue 15 had a small piece on McGoohan in its 'Star Spot' series, while issues 39, 40, 44 and 49 had little snippets about the series contained within the editorial pages.

Detail from 'Charlie's Choice' story.

The Prisoner did feature in one comic strip. In the issued dated 2 March 1968, the comic *Smash*, as part of its regular strip 'Charlie's Choice', would feature No. 6 with artwork by Brian Lewis. The strip features a young boy named Charlie who has a magical television set, whereby characters from various TV series were able to leave the TV set and enter the real world. Previous issues featured Mrs Peel, the men from U.N.C.L.E., etc. In this particular issue it just happens to be No. 6.

TV Listing Magazines

The Prisoner featured on the cover of 30 September–6 October 1967 issue of the *TV Times*, launching the series. During the series run, five other editions of the *TV*

TV Times cover. (© Rick Davy, www.theunmutual.co.uk)

TV World cover. (Jaz Wiseman)

Times carried features on McGoohan and *the Prisoner*: those for 14–20 October 1967, 28 October–3 November 1967, 25 November 25–1 December 1967, 9–15 December 1967 and 10–16 February 1968.

It also appeared on the cover of two issues of *TV World*, the first for the week of the 22–29 September. The UK premiere was in the Midlands, with the first episode showing on 29 September. In the USA the *St Louis Post Dispatch* magazine 26 May–1 June issue had a cover for the series showing over there.

Records

A theme single for the series was released on the RCA label in 1967 (RCA 1635). While this release was from the theme's composer Ron Grainer, this is a very different recording to the one used on the series, being instead a very slow harpsichord re-recording of the theme tune. The records b side was called 'Happening Sunday'. Though on this original release the

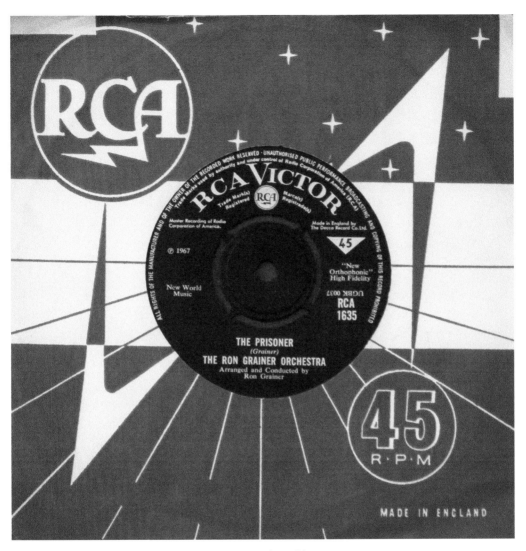

Theme single. (© Rick Davy, www.theunmutual.co.uk)

track is titled 'The Prisoner', the tracks actual title is 'The age of Elegance' and this is the title that was used on its re-release as a flexi-disc by Six of One in 1987.

This same recording was apparently used on a 1969 compilation album of TV themes put out by RCA in 1969, though this has not been verified.

Trading Cards

The firm FKS published a series of cards, or picture stamps, in 1968. The title of this set was 'The Wonderful World of Pop & TV Stars'. The set, containing 240 cards, featured several points of interest for *The Prisoner* fans, with images not only of Patrick McGoohan but also Alexis Kanner. To go with the set was a nicely presented album to store them.

In 1974 a set of 300 Artistas cards were released in Spain. McGoohan's image featured on some cards within the set and also on the individual packs.

Left: *The Wonderful World of Pop & TV Stars* album. (Phil Caunt)

Below: McGoohan cards from set. (Phil Caunt)

PAUL McCARTNEY
PAUL McCARTNEY
DOUG McCLURE
PATRICK McGOOHAN
PATRICK McGOOHAN
PATRICK McGOOHAN

ALEXIS KANNER

Alexis Kanner card. (Phil Caunt)

Artistas empty card pack.
(© Rick Davy, www.theunmutual.
co.uk)

Miscellaneous Items

As with *Danger Man*, the theme for *The Prisoner* also appeared as sheet music, with the theme being published with a photo cover by New World Music Ltd in 1967.

ATV produced their own company newsletter, which was circulated among ATV staff members. Vol. 8 No. 2 from February 1968 of this advised them on how to deal with correspondence from viewers relating to the series.

The Prisoner, like *Danger Man*, had studio fan cards produced for the series, which once again were obtainable by writing into the studio.

In 1967 during the filming of *The Prisoner* Patrick McGoohan had produced and sent out an specially designed *Prisoner* themed Christmas card. Originals of this are highly sought after, but these, like many other items, have been reproduced over years by the fan clubs.

Highly prized among collectors of the series are original production items, whether it be items used on the show, production paperwork or publicity materials including the press or publicity brochures that were produced by the studio to promote and sell the series. With so little having been produced commercially at the time for *The Prisoner*, these types of ephemera almost seem to hold more of a significance for this show than perhaps they do for other series.

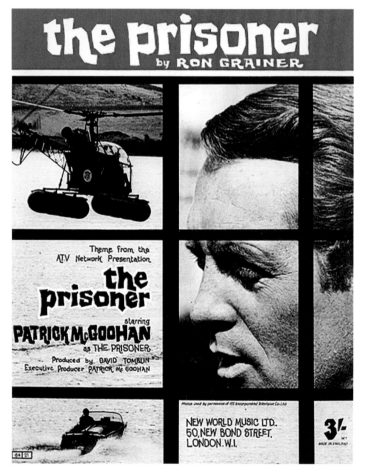

Sheet music. (© Rick Davy, www.theunmutual.co.uk)

Staff Newspaper of ATV NETWORK Ltd.

Vol. 8 No. 2   Price 3d.   February, 1968

ATV SHOWS SCORE IN '67

O UR TV coverage of the Royal Variety Show—produced for TV by Bill Ward and directed by Albert Locke—attracted not only the biggest TV audience of 1967 but also the biggest for any single channel programme... a whopping 11,600,000 homes.

This record success was revealed last month in figures giving the Top Twenty Shows for 1967. They were prepared by TAM.

Other ATV productions to score with viewers last year: the London Palladium Show on December 3 with 9,950,000 homes; "Market in Honey Lane" (April 9) with 8,850,000 homes; "Morecambe and Wise Show" (November 12) with 8,700,000 homes; "Mrs Thursday" (February 26) with 8,600,000 homes and "Secombe and Friends" (October 15) with 8,300,000 homes.

Producers of these shows were:

London Palladium Show: Albert Locke (Third in TAM's Top Twenty for 1967).

Market in Honey Lane: John Cooper (Sixth in TAM's Top Twenty for 1967).

Morecambe and Wise Show: Colin Clews (Ninth in TAM's Top Twenty for 1967.)

Mrs Thursday: Jack Williams (Tenth in TAM's Top Twenty for 1967).

Secombe and Friends: Jon Scoffield (Twelfth in TAM's Top Twenty for 1967).

by ATV REPORTER

Other statistics released by TAM last month showed that we had three series in the Top Ten Dramatic Series.

These were "Mrs Thursday" (6,550,000 homes); "Man in a Suitcase" (5,400,000 homes) and "The Prisoner" (5,400,000 homes). Patrick McGoohan's brilliant and controversial series.

CONFUSED PUBLIC

"The Prisoner" was indeed controversial. During and immediately after the London transmission on Sunday, February 4, the ATV Duty Officer logged well over 150 calls—in the main from a confused public. The following day the mail began to flood in. Strangely enough, the trends of the previous evening were reversed with a heavy correspondence in favour of the series.

Below, one of our correspondents gives his personal views on the series and explains what "The Prisoner" meant to him.

PENETRATING STUDY

"What's it all about, Patrick? This question was posed by many puzzled viewers who, fattened on a diet of pre-digested television, found thinking for themselves something of a strain. The press were more cautious—their reactions mixed.

"Was it all hokum? Has Patrick McGoohan taken us all for a ride or was this the most penetrating study—the most vivid of comments on modern civilisation—in the history of British television?

"The answer, like many aspects of the series, is all in the mind. For example, one may look at an abstract painting and draw from it one's own conclusions. The conclusions I drew from 'The Prisoner'—particularly the last episode—were disturbing and frustrating to me personally. Disturbing because, in my interpretation, they reflected my own innermost emotions—frustrating because, unlike Patrick McGoohan, I am not clever enough to find an outlet for those emotions.

MESSAGE

"A message came through to me. Whether or not the message I got was the one Mr McGoohan intended, I do not know, but 'The Prisoner' made me think. It made thousands of people think—and it made tens of thousands of people talk. Patrick McGoohan has forcefully shaken the viewing public out of its state of mental lethargy.

"What did 'The Prisoner' mean to me? Here I give my personal interpretation in the form of a plain man's guide to 'The Prisoner'."

The Village:	It did not exist in any materialistic form. It symbolised the prison that is man's own mind.
The Numbers, No. 6, etc.	This represents man's lack of freedom—the stifling of individual liberty by authority.
The Balloon—Rover:	Symbolises repression and the guardianship of corrupt authority which, when corruption is finally overcome, disintegrates.
The Penny-Farthing:	Represents the slowness of progress in our modern civilisation.
The "Hippy" Character (as played by Alexis Kanner):	Symbolises youth in rebellion against the establishment and, as in the closing sequence of the young man trying to thumb a lift first in one direction and then in another on a motorway, youth not knowing, or caring, in which direction it goes.
The Former No.2 (as played by Leo McKern):	A former trusted member of the establishment who, having broken away, is accused of having bitten the hand that fed him and is being made by authority to pay for his failures.
The Little Butler:	He represents the little men of every community, prepared to follow faithfully, like sheep, any established leader.
The "break-out" sequence, guns firing—overlaid by the theme "love, love, love":	This was a protest against the paradoxes which exist in modern civilisation. Man, preaching love, love, love against the holocaust of war. A penetrating comment on the world situation—Vietnam, the Middle East, etc.
No. 1:	The unveiling of No. 1 as Patrick McGoohan himself is representative of every man's desire to be No. 1—to be the top dog.
The "shouting-down" of McGoohan by the hooded assembly:	The inability of the ordinary man to make his voice heard—to put forward his viewpoint to the world.

Patrick McGoohan directs Alexis Kanner in a scene from "Fall Out", the controversial final episode of "The Prisoner".

ATV Newsheet. (© Rick Davy, www.theunmutual.co.uk)

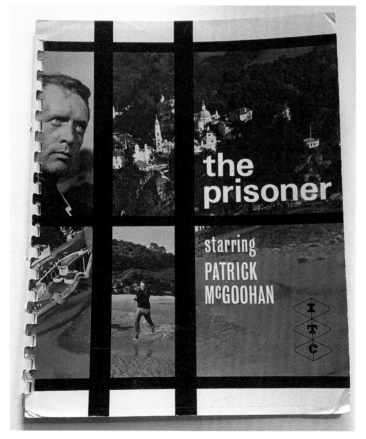

Above left: ITC fan card. (Bernard Dunne)

Above right: Christmas card.

Left: ITC Press brochure. (© Rick Davy, www.theunmutual. co.uk)